© Aladdin Books Ltd 2001

Designed and produced by
Aladdin Books Ltd
28 Percy Street
London W1P 0LD

First published in
the United States in 2001 by
Copper Beech Books,
an imprint of
The Millbrook Press
2 Old New Milford Road
Brookfield, Connecticut 06804

ISBN 0-7613-2461-5 (lib. bdg.)
ISBN 0-7613-2330-9 (paper ed.)

Cataloging-in-Publication data is on
file at the Library of Congress

Coordinator
Jim Pipe

Design
Flick, Book Design and Graphics

Picture Research
Brian Hunter Smart

Illustration
Mary Lonsdale for SGA

Picture Credits
Abbreviations: t – top, m – middle, b –
bottom, r – right, l – left, c – center.
All photographs supplied by Select Pictures
except: Cover, 2tl, 4tl, 5, 6tl, 8-9, 13, 16-17,
18tl, 20tl, 20-21, 22l, 22br, 23tl – Digital
Stock. 10tl, 16tl, 19, 24r, 24b – Corbis
Royalty Free. 7 – John Foxx Images. 8tl –
Stockbyte. 12tl – Geoff Moon; FLPA/CORBIS.
15 – Ray Bird/FLPA-Images of Nature. 24tl –
S Johnson/FLPA-Images of Nature.

My World

Rain or Shine

By Dr. Alvin Granowsky

Copper Beech Books
Brookfield, Connecticut

Weather

What is the weather today?

Some days it rains.

Some days it shines.

Some days it does both!

Gina's mom likes rain *and* shine.

Her plants need both to grow.

Hot and cold

What is the weather?

Some days are hot. Gina wears shorts and a shirt. She wishes she was at the beach!

Some days are cold. Gina wears lots of clothes. Everything is icy.

Sun

What is the weather?

It is sunny. Gina and Carlos like to play in the sun.

Gina's cat likes the sun, too.

But her dog likes the shade.

It pants to keep cool.

Clouds

What is the weather?

It is cloudy. We see fluffy
white clouds on sunny days.
Gray clouds may bring rain.

Gina and Carlos like to
watch the clouds.
What shapes can you see?

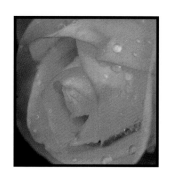

Rain

What is the weather?

It is raining. First there are a few small drops. Then it pours. Carlos and Gina love puddles!

Some people use an umbrella
in the rain.

It keeps them dry!

Wind

What is the weather?

It is windy. The wind blows Carlos' boat across the water.

12

You can feel the wind in your hair.
You can hear it in the trees.

Can you see the wind?

Storm

What is the weather?

There is a storm. The wind blows hard. The rain pours and pours.

A big wind can blow down trees.

A big rain can flood the streets.

Thunder and lightning

What is the weather?

It is a thunderstorm.

The thunder goes BOOM!

Lightning flashes across the sky.

Gina loves the storm, but the noise scares her dog.

Snow

What is the weather?

It is snowing. It is very cold outside.
Gina and Carlos play on their sled.

A big snowstorm is called a blizzard.
Some cars get stuck in the snow.

Rainbow

What is the weather?

Sometimes it rains *and* shines.

The sun shines through the rain and makes a beautiful rainbow in the sky.

Here are some kinds of weather.

Sunny

Windy

Rainy

Snow

Cloudy

22

Here are some weather words.

Lightning

Hot

Puddle

Umbrella

Can you write a story with these words?

Do you know?

Some storms are very big.

Some winds
spin very fast.

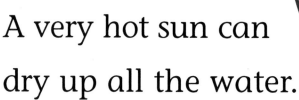

A very hot sun can
dry up all the water.